MW00412515

Positive Shift Ahead!

Positive Shift Ahead!

If things aren't going your way,
redirect yourself!

16 ways to redirect negative
thoughts quickly

Stacie René

ISBN: 9781688757318

For information regarding special discounts for bulk
purchases, please contact 248-821-5119
or email: stacie@positiveshiftahead.com.

Printed in the U.S.A.

Reader acknowledges that this Positive Shift Ahead book
does not involve the diagnosis or treatment of mental
disorders as defined by the American Psychiatric Association
and that this book is not to be used as a substitute for
counseling, psychotherapy, psychoanalysis, mental health
care, substance abuse treatment, or other professional
advice by legal, medical or other qualified professionals and
that it is the readers exclusive responsibility to seek such
independent professional guidance as needed.

Dear Reader:

We are all faced with unexpected, disruptive life changes. This is a book you can grab in your busy life and immediately make changes in your behavior that support your actions and thoughts.

It's meant to be a simple guide and starting point to change your mindset while, moving you in a better, more positive direction.

It will show you that with your thoughts becoming things, your goals, dreams, wants and desires are truly possible with the outcome you want.

You can't lead a positive life with a negative mind.

Stacie René

P.S. Please share with me your experiences of shifting your mindset and taking back control of your outcomes. I would enjoy receiving your feedback.

Visit www.stacierene.com or email me at: stacie@positiveshiftahead.com.

P.P.S. Yes, in case you are wondering, the asterisk over the é is specifically put there by my mom. She always said and knew I was special.

Contents

Contents

Foreword

"Oh, I get by with a little help from my friends
Mmm, gonna try with a little help from my
friends."

John Lennon and Paul McCartney made these lyrics famous, and many of us truly believe them. In this book, Positive Shift Ahead, Stacie Rene talks to the reader like a friend who really cares.

As an executive coach, I appreciate how she provides bite size chunks of actionable coaching on topics that are universal and does it in a way that makes the reader feel like we aren't alone. In fact, Stacie shares her own struggles, and how the coaching she provides helped her.

I will refer to this book over and over again, as life's struggles present themselves, finding coaching, guidance and real actions to help me with life's struggles like that friend that John and Paul wrote about!

Acknowledgments

I must express my very profound gratitude to my parents, Neal Mohowitsch and Ruthie Feagles, who have led me down the path of positivity and are continuously teaching me about life. You've supported all of my journeys, taught me about working hard and never letting obstacles get in the way of my goals. Appreciating that I wouldn't take "no" for an answer. When I would fail it wasn't presented as a failure but a learning experience. As people tore me down, (which was often) you were right there to bring me up, reminding me not to be like those tyrants. Most importantly, you are my biggest champions who believe in me no matter what and support me to my fullest. I will continue to shine thanks to you and everything that you have taught me.

To my husband Craig Zotkovich, my daughter Samantha and son Zachary for providing me with unfailing support and continuous encouragement throughout my years of work and through the process of finding my passion and believing in me. This accomplishment would not have been possible without you all. Sam and Zach, my most favorite is your, "Go Mommy Go!" and Craig, my biggest de-stressor is your, "We will make it work!" Thank you for being an intricate part of my life as I continue to embark on new journeys.

To my personal mentors who have guided me during my career and aided in my success. I am where I am today because you cared enough to believe in me. Giving me leadership skills, confidence and taking me under your wings; personally, and professionally. Mary Carter, Lynn Torossian and Karen Fordham, thank you for having confidence and seeing something special in me.

Thank you all, for what you have given me and for your continuous support. I couldn't have imagined writing this book without the influences each and every one of you have had on me. I am forever grateful for the part you played in instilling my confidence, strength and purpose.

The completion of this book could not have been possible without the support, participation and assistance of so many people, whose names may not all be enumerated. Their contributions are sincerely appreciated and gratefully acknowledged.

What Others are Saying About Positive Shift Ahead!

This Positive Shift Ahead book is a wonderful example of positive energy! The readers can easily transform their negative behaviors and take back their power. This book has changed my focus and I'm confident it will have a great impact on the mindset of those reading it. I'll reference this book often to keep my mindset on the right path.

Kam Carman
Detroit Broadcaster / Media Producer
Former Reporter and News Anchor for Fox 2

The Positive Shift Ahead book offers a positive approach to the way one looks at and lives their life. Reminding us that we have more control than we think. This book provides the tools to be our best self and live a life filled with greatness. Truly one of the most positive, encouraging and inspiring books I have read in years!

Jody "Mo" Mohowitsch
Owner / Publisher of Thunder Roads
Magazine of Michigan

What an energetic drive this book offers. An enthusiasm that is contagious. The ability to positively shift you to a new level. Stacie teaches an effective approach on positive thinking. Enlightens your mindset toward awareness and reflection. This book encourages individual growth and cultural change within an organization.

Curt Lawson
Police Executive / Law Enforcement

Stacie is one of those people you meet and never forget. Beautiful both inside and outside, she's like a butterfly... landing in your life for a short time to share her joy, and then moving on to make others smile. In her book, she shares her secrets for maintaining a positive attitude and using life's setbacks as an opportunity to grow. I applaud Stacie for putting her voice into words so that others may learn. Don't miss this read. You'll be inspired!

Mary Carter
President, Learning Designs, Inc.

This book reviews and summarizes simple steps to getting yourself unstuck. It works as a good introduction to self-development and thinking differently. I see why Stacie made this a quick and easy "airplane" read with relatable real-life experiences, yet simple situations we all go though.

Rhonda Cerone
Business Entrepreneur / Realtor

It's REAL. Shifting my mindset was
. something I didn't even realize I needed, until
I read Positive Shift Ahead! Reading this
book and working with Stacie, we uncovered
ways to keep my mindset where it needed to
be. When you read this book, your energy
operates on a different frequency and your life
possibilities become endless. This book has
been a pivotal part of my life for personal and
business growth. It is a perfect guide to
redirect quickly and getting you on the right
path!

Chad Ever
Ever Studios CEO
Websites / Consulting / Advertising

The Positive Shift Ahead book teaches an effective approach on positive thinking. Stacie explores real life situations with examples of shifting your thinking from negative to positive. Optimism will ensure that you respond to those negative life events in the most positive mindset that will lead to positive outcomes. Stacie's Positive Shift shows that people who succeed aren't the ones who avoid failure; they are the ones who learn how to respond to failure and life's obstacles with a positive mind. A positive mind is a powerful mind. This is a must read!

Heather Burrows
Fit4U Owner and Business Entrepreneur

Stacie René

Introduction

Positive Shift Ahead was designed to give you the keys or combination to unlock and break the chains that bind all people. The bind that victimizes us because of our own self-doubt, insecurities, never feeling good enough and always trying to keep up with this fast-paced world today.

Life is about ups and downs and knowing how to handle those situations... getting a grip on your negativity, insecurities and depressive state before it starts to affect you. Stop it before it becomes your new personality and habit.

The "up" times are most often the easiest. Why? Because you're stable, your income is good, you're surrounded by success. Your feelings are flowing positively and freely; you are in full-speed ahead mode. You're exuberant and allowing all the good positive emotions to flow in.

During those "down" moments is where your growth starts to take place. What are you going to change, what are you going to make a difference in, and how are you going to find yourself again? When your bubble bursts and you are knocked down, you need to step back and appreciate the reasoning for "why" it is happening, how you're going to handle the situation and again, grow from it.

When I was facing challenges and was even brought to my knees, hands on my face and tears rolling down my cheeks...I knew I had to change it. I couldn't continue feeling and living those horrible emotions. It took over every thought I had and every action I took. It consumed my whole body so I felt like I was vibrating with negativity. That is when I knew, at that moment, I was going to take back my own emotions, feelings and thoughts. Stand up and say NO MORE! I'm mentally, emotionally and physically taking my control back.

The question is: How do you get stuck or get in that situation? The answer is simple: It creeps up on you or it just happens over time. Before you know it, you're not yourself anymore, things that were funny aren't, and the things you loved doing or who you were now feel insignificant. Maybe you have experienced a job loss, a divorce, a demotion at work, or were deceived by someone you trusted. You've become complacent, no goals set and the list could go on. After that, you often seek revenge and are scorned by the difficult situation and constantly feel life isn't fair. In the present and in the future, you carry "revenge/anger" on to every experience. That makes you stuck. FORGIVE AND GROW. Focus and develop you. Work on yourself continuously.

1

Self-Identity, Knowing Who YOU Are

The more you know who you are, and what you want, the less you let things upset you.

Getting to know yourself better

"Who am I?" A question we have all been trying to find the answer to. A question that was born with us and will haunt us till our very last breath. In a question paper, all of us have an answer to each question asked except when it says, describe yourself in a few words. It's much harder to describe or talk about yourself, yet we can easily describe other people with no problem.

Knowing yourself better is something that goes far beyond the normal. It isn't just about knowing your favorite colors or your best music or even your favorite artist. No! It is something much bigger than that. We seem to know more about celebrities' lives, marriage, likes/dislikes, styles, and what they are eating than we know about ourselves. Looking at the big picture; we don't always know, understand or even respect ourselves like we should.

Self-identity is a unique process that involves YOU learning and understanding "you" better. By "you," I mean the individual human you are at a way deeper level - not just the surface.

This journey to self-identity is one that isn't exactly pleasant, but you must be very willing to embark on it. You will meet all your insecurities, all your doubts, all your attitudes and behaviors. It is something that gives you the ability to consider seriously the way you live and how you live.

To be frank with you, this process can actually suck and feel stupid when you begin. But with time it gets better, of course, with hard work and diligence. At the end of the day, to better understand who you are, what you want and how to go about things that concern you is a huge step in the right direction.

Properly knowing and understanding who you really are means: you now pay attention to your life values. Attention to your beliefs, moods, body, numerous habits (good and bad). Basically, it's knowing and understanding what make you function.

At this stage of self-identity, you better understand what moves you specifically are making throughout the day. Goals, desires, passions idiosyncrasies and dreams are in better perspective. It's important to continuously respect and work on yourself as a human being. This quest makes you better determine what you want in life and gives you the strength to work towards that.

It is important to know that no one is born knowing themselves. We all come to learn more about ourselves as we grow older.

Lying to ourselves

All of us have been trying to create an identity for ourselves. So, when someone asks, "who are you?" or "what do you do?" or something about us, we have an answer to it. We are trying to create an identity in front of people we know and for the people we don't. Where everyone is too busy thinking about themselves, there is hardly anyone going to think about you...and yet we happily spend most of our day thinking what people think of us.

Here's the truth, though. What you think others think of you is actually what you think about yourself. We are all the mirrors of our own thoughts. We are trying to create an image of ourselves in front of others and we are counting the deeds to push that image up further. This helps us see a version of our own self and place it in a category of people we probably don't belong with, creating a fake self-identity for our self.

Know more about your core values

Core values are those moral codes you hold truly high in your heart. Every individual has their own set of core values and it's what defines us. These values play a major role in our life's daily activities - in our ability to influence others, to persuade, to communicate, and to make decisions.

To better understand your core values, ask yourself about the things you can never compromise in your house, in your work place, at school. Those are your core values.

Perhaps it's honesty, being dedicated to a course, the ability to be flexible in decisions, wisdom? These things make you who you are. Are you someone who values responsibility? Or, do you shy away from it?

Once you can determine these things, they will help you better process the best life path to thread.

You are someone

We are all so busy grinding to build ourselves that we are lost in the activities we perform daily. We rush to the office and then back home. Grind at the gym, cook in the kitchen, hang out with people we don't want to be with, try to impress someone who won't even look back at us, and then mourn about how hard it is to live a good life. Overwhelmed in the work and running short of time, by the end of the day we forget who we are. We forget that we are "someone."

You are what you do; You are what you think

There are things you do now and they define who you are now. Self-identity is not limited to things that exist now, however. There is a lot more to it. It also includes who you think you are. We want to be someone, do things in life and have goals. All these are not related to who you are right now, but who you want to be. Each thing we do today is what defines us for the tomorrow.

Understanding your dreams

We all know that our dreams and hopes are what gives us a future to hold. With them, you can start and live the life you've always wanted. Just know that your dreams matter a lot. They are very important and are worth your time chasing after them. Because of this, it's a good idea to know more about them. Find out more details and specifics about what you want.

Do you want to become an athlete? Ask yourself what kind. Do you want to be a football player? What position will you play? Or is it a musician you dream of becoming? Find out more about the instrument you want to play. To what level do you want your dream to take you? Do you have the zeal and dedication (core values) to keep it alive?

Once you make your dreams an integral part of your daily struggle, you can begin to take them more seriously. Work on them properly and bring them out to light.

Until then...Don't Coast in Neutral, Positive Shift Ahead!

2

Paying Attention to the Signs

How will you know if it's the right decision if you never make it.

Sometimes we get nudges throughout the day. It may be something we see, hear, or read. It makes us think for a moment and then we move on to what we were previously doing. Then, we may see, hear, or read the same thing again an hour, a day, or a week later. It makes us stop and think but— once again—we move on to what we were doing. After you see, hear, or read the same thing for the third or fourth time, you really should stop and ask yourself, "Why does this subject keep coming up? If one more person says this, or if I read this/see this again then perhaps it might be a sign." However,

9

inevitably, you stay in your pattern of routine and continue ignoring these nudges that are right in front of you.

Sometimes we pay attention to these nudges, and sometimes we don't. Sometimes we take action; most times we don't. It's interesting, though, if we don't pay attention, the nudges don't go away! For example, when you're given hints to slow down and you ignore them, you may get a figurative slap-in-the-face to get your attention.

This happened to me several times. The first time, I got a stress migraine, then another one that lasted for five days, but I continued to push myself. The second time, my husband told me that he could see what was happening and I was doing it again, over booking, not saying no, and things are slipping that need to be done. I, of course, ignored his comment – along with comments from friends who said I looked tired, stressed and asked if I was okay. Even while driving, always rushing to get to the next thing...I got a speeding ticket.

Nothing was stopping me. I thought I knew better, so though I'm running on empty and received several nudges to slow down, I keep pushing. The next thing you know…I walked into the bathroom, there were a few drops of water on the floor, I wobbled and broke two toes. Snap! Yep, that simple.

Another time, after ignoring nudges to slow down, I was finishing a workout at the gym. My heel came down on a dumbbell that was on the ground. I broke my foot in two spots and tore three ligaments. Another wakeup call!

Apparently, I am a slow learner because that wasn't all that happened Despite several "Slow Down" nudges, I still didn't listen. The next one got my attention. I was running around the kitchen trying to get things done going a mile a minute and all of a sudden, I was on the floor and apparently tried to do the splits. The results were close to a stage 3 hamstring tear; which meant I was near surgery. This one took me out for almost a year and was my biggest wakeup call to slow down.

What if we start paying attention to the nudges and respond intentionally? This requires taking a chance, perhaps choosing the path less clear—the one with more branches and cobwebs in the way, and yet might have a brighter, more successful outlet at the end. The nudges are there because the current wide-open clear path with no obstacles, your comfortable routine, is making you feel unsuccessful day after day.

What if you respond intentionally, try the new path and discover it isn't what you want? Respond intentionally! This isn't a wrong decision or a failure, it just wasn't the path for you; you would have never known that had you not tried. I'll bet you will learn new things along the way that will help you on your next path. I've stepped into that situation a few times with no regrets. Just keep in check with who you are - your core values, your passions, and what is important to you.

After several slaps, I started to listen, be observant and take notice of the nudges. No one has time to stop and slow down; I had no choice when I was limping around injured. The steamrollers of life will come and get us. That was clear and evident to me. I'm sure you can relate to my situation.

Your big slap might be a health scare, relationship breakdown, or many other things. Sure, these can be hard and dark times, but in the end, they can be the best things that happen to us.

What decisions, nudges or actions are you ignoring? How can you choose to respond intentionally? Be more aware of these things and you will be surprised about what happens. Enjoy the journey of the unknown; you might just like it.

Until then...Don't Coast in Neutral, Positive Shift Ahead!

3

Beating Self-Doubt

Your life isn't yours if you always care what others think.

As you go throughout your day, when is the last time you stopped to think...what's my next chapter in life? If not, why not? If so, what's your plan? Is it your own personal self-doubt, not knowing what to do next or is it your negative thoughts that may be prohibiting you from moving forward?

It doesn't matter what your age is or where you are in life. A lot of us wake up every morning and aren't sure where we're going in life or what's next. The world is constantly changing and giving us challenges—especially when we are comparing ourselves to each other, living up

15

Stacie René

to others' expectations and putting unnecessary pressure on ourselves. Stop looking around, comparing yourself to everyone else, and get a new goal or chapter figured out.

That's how I felt when I had been wanting to write a book. I actually had written four books and let them sit in my computer for years and years because I didn't know how to move forward with them. I was also doubting my books and wondering if anyone would find value in them. I finally worked up the courage to print my elementary book and have the principal where my children attended read it. Not only did she find it positive, inspiring and what the children needed to learn about, but she insisted I write another series for the older kids in the school. Floored and taken back by her honesty and feedback, I decided to take it a step further and read it to my son' 1st grade class. It was a success! One student said he loved the book but was disappointed he wasn't in there and

16

asked if I could add him as a character. Since then, word got around and the teachers asked when I could come to their class and read the book next.

Self-doubt is a limiting and unnecessary feeling, yet we all partake in it quite heavily. When it came to actually making this move forward and go to editing, I froze. Reread every chapter, over analyzing everything and more. Enough already! I used the CCD and mantra every single time I would feel insecure or doubt myself... not allowing negative thoughts in and changed them to.... this is going to be my best book ever! Everyone has and always will have their own opinion and you can't please everyone.

Moving forward, let's make it easy and focus on two things. When you are self-doubting yourself or holding back from fear, start using Cancel, Clear, Delete (CCD). Those three words should be used when you're doubting yourself, having negative thoughts or feeling wishy-washy. Say the CCD three times over and over and over. Then say a mantra you can easily remember. Here's one to get you started: Every day in every way, I am better, better and BETTER! Another simple mantra you can use is: I AM awesome, successful and smart; I succeed at what I put my mind to!

If you use these two simple steps (CCD and Mantra) every time you have self-doubt or a negative thought, it will change your mindset. If you have to say the CCD and Mantra 100 times a day to retrain your mind, that's totally fine.

Why do this, you ask? It's simple; the CCD and Mantra gets you to stop the negative thought and self-doubt because you are saying the CCD and Manta. It gives you time to refocus and get your mind back on track. Now, shift gears, go for your goals and use the Positive Shift of the CCD and Mantra to move you forward!

Until then...Don't Coast in Neutral, Positive Shift Ahead!

4

Your Life Changing Coach

It's okay to invest in yourself and put yourself first. It will be your biggest return on investment.

Are you going backwards in life? Maybe just wandering and not going anywhere? What about moving throughout your day and just existing? It's time to Positive Shift Ahead — make new goals and have a new outlook in your life, both personally and professionally, if that fits your circumstances.

Most of us will spend money on things, but what about spending money on yourself? It is definitely time to invest in yourself to move forward. The results may just make you blossom with a clearer mind and less haunting baggage. If this is exactly what you need for a healthier you, then find a life or personal coach. Personal coaches can help you get past difficult obstacles and create strategies to unlock your potential. They show you how to redirect yourself and move towards your goals. Much like this book.

It's the same thing as taking a college class, only you are investing in yourself and your career. Coaching will help you better yourself, and that leads to advances in your personal life and career. Personal coaches are more accepted in today's society. More businesses and their management support their employees because they are seeing a significant difference in those employees with business, personal and life coaches — so much that some are even paying for it! There are workable solutions to increase self-worth, goal setting, and personal organization.

I, too, struggled with this wondering why anyone would spend money on a personal coach. After months of deliberation and listening to a motivational talk, I finally decided it was time and went for it. Using my theory that I had nothing to lose, but more importantly, everything I could gain from it, I wouldn't know if I didn't try. Much to my surprise, the success I gained was life changing. Coaching opened my eyes to my personal strength, things I internally had buried and suppressed, and it allowed me to break down my insecurities that were built up over the years. Since then, I embarked on my own company, became an author, didn't shy away from confrontation and had many more takeaways from that experience.

This could be the answer you're looking for to make a change in your life. Solutions to issues and problems lingering in your current situation can be addressed. There are other things that can be remedied, as well.

Your mind is a useful and powerful tool; remember, today's thoughts become tomorrow's reality. If you know how to properly use the tools you are given, you have nothing to lose and everything to gain.

The more you use it, the faster it comes, and the happier you will feel!

Until then…Don't Coast in Neutral, Positive Shift Ahead!

5

What and Who Are You Appreciating Today

*Learn to appreciate the things you have,
before time forces you to appreciate the things
you once had.*

Having a tough start to your day? Stop what you are doing and take a moment to think about something that makes you smile or happy. If you cannot think of anything now, be happy that you woke up, can breathe on your own, have vision to see the beauty around you, or that even if you sometimes have to fake a smile, you actually have the ability.

We are so used to our surroundings that we fail to see how far we've come and what we've accomplished. I wasn't born with all

23

the bells and whistles and an unlimited cash flow. I always wanted what other people had and felt that name brand materialist things were a must. However, my parents did the best they could and provided us four kids with meals on the table, clothes, toys and as much else as possible.

As a child, I learned to work hard and believe in myself. Working hard to be somebody. Working hard to be somebody. I recall one time this woman stopped me to tell me I had the most beautiful hair she had ever seen. I said thank you and went on my way. Little did she know that I was so mad my hair didn't turn out perfectly that day. The angrier I got, the worse my hair looked; I finally screamed, I WISH I WAS BALD! Really... over a hair style? I never took into account that maybe she had gone through an experience and lost her hair or something else. I didn't appreciate my thick, beautiful hair and in turn I was striving for perfection.

Today, I would give anything to have that natural brunette, no grey, thick glossy hair.

I also took for granted that I could run around, jump on trampolines and laugh hard all without peeing my pants. Now, I have to know where the bathroom is everywhere, use the restroom before I go running, and pray that I make it to the 4.7-mile marker to use the restroom and be careful with my belly laughs. Oh, what I wish I would have back!

Along those lines is my eyesight. Having perfect 20/20 vision was a norm for me. Getting older and in my forties, I noticed some slight visual challenges but nothing major. As I turned 46, something changed and I mean drastically. all of a sudden, I couldn't see my text messages, emails or even my running watch without blurriness. I called the ophthalmologist and told them I needed to come in again, something is terribly wrong. Even though I was there three months ago. Maybe I had a tumor, and yes, I was totally catastrophizing. Needless to say, he proclaimed it to be my age and it was time to stop fighting it and get some glasses.

These days, I'm more attuned to the things around me and appreciate everything around me. At night before I go to bed, I say all the things that come to my mind that I appreciate and am grateful for. Simple things such as the bed I'm sleeping in, my job, salary, car, clothes, my looks, my health, family, children, friends, the opportunity or obstacle that I was presented with that day and people I met; the list can go on and on.

Remember to be grateful for these and the other little things sometimes taken for granted, as they can be taken away in a blink of an eye and others may be pining for these abilities, they no longer are able to enjoy.

Sometimes, we all need to take a step back and appreciate the small things! So, start today by sending a text to a friend or family member, letting them how happy you are to have them in your life. It could change not only your day, but also theirs!

Ask yourself every morning what are you grateful for today and one positive thing that is going to happen to you today. Try asking those two questions to your friends and family to see what they say. It's a rewarding feeling and sets a positive tone to your day!

Until then...Don't Coast in Neutral, Positive Shift Ahead!

6

Being in Control of Your Emotions

Emotions are a temporary state of mind, don't let them permanently destroy you.

To live a better and happier life, you must take charge of the natural instinctive state of your mind arising from circumstances, moods or relationships with others.

Controlling your emotions doesn't mean ignoring them; it means you recognize and take rightful action on them. You must be in charge of your emotions day-to-day. If you truly desire unlimited happiness, controlling your emotions is a necessity. A clear mind leads to controlled emotions. Unclutter your mind.

Yes, obstacles come up in life. If you're in the situation of having an unstable job, an

unfaithful partner, experiencing stubborn
children, nagging co-workers, or the know-it-
all people you come in contact with, it can
easily try your patience. An uncontrolled state
of mind can make a bad situation worse,
particularly if you already have a lot going on
and are frustrated.

Every emotion begins with a thought. If
you can learn to control your thoughts, you
can take charge of your emotions which leads
to a more productive and less stressful day. It
does take practice and isn't easy at first.
Think of it as an airplane. Airplanes don't just
simply turn around. It takes a very large turn
and takes time to fully make the turn. Just
like your thoughts. It will take some time to
readjust and be in control of your emotions.
The key here i the more you catch yourself
from getting angry, emotional and lashing
out, the more control you have of those
particular feelings. They characterize the state
of your mind, such as hate, anger, fear,
happiness, jealousy, or love.

Think about all the success you experience or feel after you've come out of a hardship. All the struggles you had and yet you overcame them and also learned some things along the way.

Years and years of past learning experiences is what develops you and your strengths. You are smarter because of those difficult times.

Without learning those lessons and hardships along the way in life, you wouldn't be where you are now. Learning about emotions helps friendship and families get though some of the toughest times. Understanding negative emotions and what we would call "cruel" people in the past will help you deal with the different personalities you may encounter with bosses, co-workers, teachers, partners, and friends throughout life.

During my personal experiences, I have to say that the thoughts and emotions I allowed to take control and put in my head were so strong that my heartrate would increase, I would get sick to my stomach and my heart felt like it was clenched. Because I was creating such strong emotions, it took my whole body over. When I was out running one day and had to get 10 miles in, I was stressed because my running partner couldn't make it. I didn't feel prepared to run it, let alone by myself. I felt insecure and awful about myself and was stressing over work issues. My internal mental conversations, thoughts and emotions took over and made me stop in my tracks because I couldn't breathe and felt like my throat was closing up from all my emotions. I burst into tears and had to walk for a bit. I had eight more miles to run and no way could I do it feeling like this. I was so caught up in my headspace that I looked around me and didn't know where I was. Totally consumed by my very thoughts, I needed to focus and redirect these destructive thoughts. I was an angry woman and it was a horrible feeling. Taking my own advice which I offer to others (using the cancel, clear, delete words on my thoughts and saying my mantra over and over) I thought of a happy place and ended up putting my hand on my heart saying: I am love, I am loved, I am loving, I am loveable. I carried on and completed my 10 miles. I must have looked ridiculous with my hand over my heart, but at that point I didn't care and it worked. The whole CCD, mantra, happy place and "I am" positive shift worked!

When you are filled with self-doubt, you may not understand how to stop your own internal bullying and negativity.

Don't let yourself be controlled by others' negativity. Be proud of who you are and stand up for yourself. Be the plane that makes that turn faster by catching yourself and stop the emotional thoughts from controlling you. You are the only one who can allow someone's negativity to affect you.

Be proud of who you are and stand up for yourself. Don't let fear hold you back. If you continue to live in a world of insecurities, you are missing out on so much of the beautiful life and closing off the good things that are meant to come your way. Living means taking risks and going beyond your comfort zone. You can't live a POSITIVE life with a negative mind.

Until then...Don't Coast in Neutral, Positive Shift Ahead!

7

What No One Wants to Talk About

It's going to happen to each and every one of us, yet we are all afraid to talk about it as if it we can run from it, but we can't.

Most would know me to have an aptitude for mentoring, educating, inspiring, encouraging, and empowering individuals to be the most extraordinary people they can be.

As you may or may not know, I am the founder of The Positive Shift; a consulting firm that does educating, strategy and motivational speaking. My company's philosophy fits perfectly with my enthusiasm for interacting with community members and educating them on all life skills.

Many community members I meet with have been through similar struggles. Still, they understand we are all connected somehow and we can come out of anything stronger than ever. It's all in how we handle each situation.

It's important to know and understand where you are in life. Planning as much as possible is vital. If you're getting married, having a baby, changing jobs, losing a loved one or celebrating a new chapter in life, you are constantly going through stages of planning the next steps of your future.

Even funeral planning – an obviously sad life event – and the situation affects each and every one of us differently.

I would have never thought of this situation or brought it up without my own experiences. On my way to work one day, I got a call from my dad letting me know my brother had just passed in a motorcycle accident. I became foggy and felt numb, not knowing what to do. I didn't believe the story my dad told me about. I drove to work, called my neighbor and close friend Fran, and asked what I was supposed to do. Thank gosh she was there, because this was a first experience for me. Sure, I lost my grandparents, but this was different. What makes me sad now is that I wish I had been more involved in the planning and process of his funeral. I knew my brother well and what he would have wanted. His funeral with him laid out in a casket was not what he would have wanted. I had to let it go but was frustrated every year around the same time he passed. Then, a few years later my mother-in-law fell ill, had emergency surgery, went to a rehab center to get better, and after about four months passed away. She lived in North Carolina, passed away in Tennessee, was cremated in Georgia and we were to have her memorial in Michigan. Talk about a HOT mess and a lot of confusions. I had to do the usual duties of planning a funeral/memorial. Had I known more about this, I again, would have done it differently.

My whole point in this chapter is to make you aware of things you would have never thought about. You really do need to consider the planning of your legacy and what you are doing to your family, friends, kids, neighbors - what they end up having to do when a loved one passes.

Since then, I ended up working at a funeral home and, as an educator, I was able to talk about things that no one wished to discuss and connected them with an advisor who could help them plan their lasting legacy, 100% their way. When we think about funeral planning, it's not as bad as we think if we are proactive and have an open mind. At one educational event at which I was presenting, I saw a woman get emotional and start to cry. After I was finished with the presentation, I approached her and asked if she was okay or if it was something I said. She said that she had been wanting to plan for this. She didn't want to have her daughter do it after she passed, but didn't know how or who to contact. She said they were tears of relief. Needless to say, I introduced her to a preplanning advisor. The day of her appointment, I picked her friend up as she wanted to be there to plan as well (but couldn't drive) and I sat with the two of them and the advisor. I have seen these two ladies at community events since then. Every single time they go out of their way to thank me. Brings me joy knowing I helped take unnecessary stress off of these ladies.

My biggest return on investment was to feel and see peoples' comfort with understanding, the process and knowledge they gained. It let me know I have done my part, especially when they come over and give me a big hug for no other reason than to say thank you. Gives me peace knowing that they don't have to experience the "unknown" and be in a fog when the situation arises. Preplanning truly is a gift you are giving everyone around you. Please just consider it and take action. You don't have to fully pay for it now, but get it preplanned in advanced. They have a wonderful personal planning guide that you can fill out on your own time. Being afraid, not talking about it or not dealing with it doesn't solve anything. You never know when it's your time as every day of life is truly a gift. Celebrate your life the way you want it to be when it's your time.

Until then...Don't Coast in Neutral, Positive Shift Ahead!

8

Kindness, Actions Speak Louder than Words

When you are kind to others, it not only changes you but it changes those around you.

When is the last time you offered some kindness to another person? How did it affect their day? How did it make you feel?

Kindness is the act of doing something for another person without the expectation of having it paid back to you. In many cases, an act of kindness cannot, in fact, be paid back.

We live in a very fast-paced world. Many of us are busy, on our way somewhere, without time to stop and do something for another person. We have so much on our minds and we continue to move though our day and the routine of our day.

We might be thinking about tomorrow's tasks or worried about what we are going to be doing tonight, dinner plans, work events, a big meeting the next morning and getting the kids (if you have them) to their destination.

Thinking about ourselves and what we have to get done and what is on our schedules. Full busy schedules. We don't even notice our surroundings anymore. Sound familiar?

In essence, we are trapped in our thoughts and emotions, where it becomes incredibly difficult to see others around us or the beauty around us. We are constantly in a state of rush, rush, rush, while encouraging ourselves to do more, more, more.

Kindness is about putting other people ahead of ourselves and taking the time to give someone else a piece of our time.

TIME! Time is so undervalued. It is one of the most valuable commodities, yet we don't offer it enough to the people who could use it the most. Voluntary, it is not something that can be taxed or stolen from us. No one controls our decision to provide quality time and kindness except ourselves.

I teach my children the importance of giving and being kind, without the person knowing. While at a restaurant one evening, the kids wanted to do a random act of kindness and choose someone. The table was selected and we told the server that we would like to pick up their tab as a kind gesture but did not want them to know. The server agreed and proceeded to make it happen. When it was our time to check out, the server came to us and told us that he had spoken to his manager about it. His manager was so taken back that he asked the server to let us know that because of our kind gesture, he would be picking up our tab and the other table's tab. We were surprised by this and told the server that wasn't what we were expecting and we really would like to do this. He said the manager insisted, and said it was nice to see that there were still thoughtful people in this world who still cared like we did. We sat there in silence, not believing this happened, and felt the appreciation that was just given to us. We all hoped that the others' whose lives we touched by doing our past and future acts of kindness would feel this fulfilled.

Another act of kindness that pulled at my heartstrings was when I worked at the hospital. I was in the pharmacy waiting for some scripts to be filled. There was a younger man there trying to pick his up, as well. He had just come from the emergency room and appeared to in rough shape. As he went to pay for his prescriptions, he realized he didn't have enough to cover the co-pay. He left there with his head down. I waited a minute, then went after him. Taking my work badge off, I tried to appear that I was just a person in the hospital. I had a $50 Visa gift card that just happened to be in my purse. I came from behind him, taped his shoulder and handed him the gift card. Told him I felt he could use this today and hoped he had a good rest of his day. He looked at me funny and broke down in tears. He wanted to know why, how, and why today. He told me he had just been mugged, his wallet and car stolen, and he wasn't having a good day. I said I hope this helps a little bit, I smiled, walked away and headed back to my office. Later that day, on my way out, I stopped back to the pharmacy to pick up the scripts I had been waiting for. The pharmacist told me he knew what I had done and it was very kind. I told him I had no idea what he was talking about, smiled, paid for my items and left. Not a word was spoken about it again.

I would challenge you to give your kindness and perhaps some time to someone. Not asking what's in it for me, but asking yourself how you can help another person. It means you should be on the lookout to fill a gap in the life of someone who may be struggling or who could use your time while not wanting anything in return.

When they say it feels good to give, it truly is satisfying and feels phenomenal.

What kind act or gesture are you able to do this week or on a weekly basis? Remember, it doesn't have to involve money. It could be that you are complimenting every person you see that day. Holding the door open for anyone with whom you come in contact. What about smiling and telling each person you see to have a terrific Tuesday? The possibilities are endless.

It's you and you alone who can take action on a random act of kindness.

If, by doing this, your heartstrings are pulled by an act of kindness, I would love to hear your story!

Until then...Don't Coast in Neutral, Positive Shift Ahead

9

Rightly focused – Want vs. Don't Want

Believe in what you want so much that it has no choice but to materialize.

The success of anything you do begins with focus. You have to understand what you want and go for it, and stop thinking about things that you don't want. Focusing is an act of will, which actually rules your wants. Think about it this way: YOU attract all the parts that work together simply by using the power of your focus and what you truly want.

Only you can create success for yourself. The more you think about your thoughts and your positive actions, you're creating success. What I mean is...the more you attract "like" thoughts and actions, the more success you are bringing into your life. Any time you want to break the habits of failure, all you have to do is hold your focus on the positive thoughts and actions and that will create success for you.

Yes, it is difficult at first as you will be drawn back to your old way of thinking and of course your past actions. That is a personality trait that you have created and it is a habit. Focusing on the negative can cause a lack of focus and failure on the positive thing you want and desire.

Lack of focus is generally cause for failure. When you are procrastinating, hesitating, dragging your feet on something, it is because you are focusing on the stuff that takes your mind away from your own personal "WANT" you are trying to achieve.

Focusing on problems causes a lack of focus on the solution. STOP IT! If you want to achieve the fastest, maximum results, keep your mind positive and focus on your wants.

How fast your success comes depends on how much you focus in the right direction versus how much you focus in the wrong direction. Focusing in the wrong direction is what causes doubt, fear and worry. No one has time for that! When you allow yourself to be distracted by other things on your mind, you will attract less power to do the work that will make you successful. Therefore, it is important to cut yourself away from unhealthy things as much as possible so you are able to fully focus and get your optimal success.

Remember to focus on your "wants" and stop focusing on the "don't wants" in your life. You have to actually believe it as well and not be wishy washy. Think of it this way. Suppose I was to put a pen down in front of you and ask you to pick it up. You lean over, pick up the pen from my desk, and hold it in your hand. You look at me wondering what that was all about. Picking up the pen was the easiest thing. You focused on picking the pen up and believing you could do it, easily. I then ask you if you picked the pen up or if you tried to pick the pen up. I'm sure you would tell me, with a confused look on your face, that you simply just picked the pen up... as if I didn't see you holding it in your hand. I then tell you that, it's just that simple... you either picked it up or you didn't pick it up. There is no trying, and you didn't have to decide to do it. You believed you could, so you did. That's also true in terms of staying focused on your wants and believing in them. Believe in yourself, believe in your wants, and believe in what you are focusing on.

Most people want things but let fear or doubt get in the way. There was no fear or doubt in picking up the pen. The inner dialogue could have sounded like: I don't want to pick it up, I'm not sure if I can pick it up, or I don't think I should pick it up...nope, you just reached over and picked up the pen. Don't lose focus of what you want or what you can do, it's that simple. Losing focus is so easy to do if you allow it. The pen thought is a good reminder to keep positivity in the forefront of what you want!

During my time of leaving the hospital, working for a home health company, trying to start my own company and not feeling positive or happy, I was in a constant negative space. I would secretly cry in the shower so no one would see me, cry in my car when I was alone, or stay in the bathroom until I could compose myself. I kept saying I can't handle this anymore, I can't do this anymore, I can't find myself anymore, I can't find my happiness. For someone who appeared to have it together on the outside, always looking well put together, I was a complete mess. Hiding it all. It was a terrifying feeling.

I won't forget the day I was on my hands and knees in my bedroom crying, on the phone saying all those feelings to my friend who just listened. After I hung the phone up, I stared out the window and had the biggest conversation with myself. I got mad and said enough already! I was focusing on all the things I didn't want; therefore, I was getting a hell of a lot more of crap or "bad" coming my way. Again, at that point, I decided no more! NO NO NO MORE! I decided from that point on, I wouldn't say, "I don't want" again and changed to all the things I wanted. Saying I was going to get a call out of the blue for a job, that good things were coming my way, all the things I was grateful for and I continued to be positive. Only room for what I wanted and what was going to come to me. My life changed at that point. I woke up with a positive thought, got a new fun manta that meant something to me, I was now in control of myself, my thoughts, my own outcome of what I wanted and my own success. I thought, believed and felt it!

To experience success, you must act and think success. You need to embody the qualities of success and allow the simple results come your way.

Start thinking positively, initiate and ignite your thoughts, and focus on your wants! The journey toward success will help you develop, be focused, be courageous, become wiser, have a stronger willpower, become more flexible and have the faith to persevere. Enjoy the benefits of focusing and being positive! If you are the problem, you must therefore be the solution.

Until then...Don't Coast in Neutral, Positive Shift Ahead

10

How You Handle Change

Change is one of the biggest fears in life. Stop being afraid of what could go wrong. Start being excited about what can go right.

Change in your life can be quite challenging. Whether it's a positive or negative change...remember, it is all in how you handle it. William Pollard once said, and I quote: "Without change there is no innovation, creativity, or incentive for improvement. Those who initiate change will have a better opportunity to manage the change that is inevitable."

If we don't like something in our personal life, we are privileged to have many opportunities to change it. People who are ready to take their future in their hands can make a decision to better their lives. Most times all we need to get going is to hear the right word—at the right time. It gets you motivated and ready to go and be successful!

Making the right decision goes a long way in changing our lives for the better. As a reminder, you can achieve anything you want in life if you are determined and focused. At times, all you need do is to get out of your comfort zone.

Accept a change that will improve your personal life or business for the better. The truth is, you can't keep doing the same thing over and over again and expect a different result. You need to take the bull by the horns and face that challenge.

You have what it takes to attain your desired dream. You are your best motivation. Know what you want and then go for it. Why settle for less? The importance of creativity can never be overemphasized. Always be conscious of the fact that not all ideas stick, but you will not know what works or doesn't work unless you try. Always strive to improve. What a great reason to embrace new ideas in business, yourself, or other things, and see how your determination and new thought process can improve your level of success.

Most successful businesses, chambers, rotaries, and charities of today at one point in time had challenges; therefore, the determination to succeed always kept them going. You should always be conscious of the fact that no one likes to fail; however, this is how we find out if it is to be successful or change is needed...most of the time great things come out of new ideas.

In your journey to success, always give respect to whom respect is due. We all need self-satisfaction, no matter what is driving us. You never know when yours will strike, so keep on trying. The truth is, nothing can distract a determined mind. Because when you are determined, you are focused and a focused person has a vision which they will reach at a particular point in time.

On the other hand, you can continually make excuses for failure, or give reasons not to do well in whatever you find yourself doing. The truth is, successful people don't give excuses, they make things happen, even when the conditions seem unfavorable. They always ensure there is a good result, even from a bad situation. They could give excuses because the process seems difficult [after all, anything can be justified]. There is a light at the end of the tunnel, they face the challenge and bring out something positive from it. You can achieve anything you want to. Nothing can limit you. The only limitation you have is yourself.

Trying to challenge myself, I decided since I was great with children and had patience's for them, why wouldn't I want to be a nanny. I started to look into it while I was still working a co-op job at the hospital and taking a few college courses. I didn't know what I wanted to do, so why not try something new? I found an agency, interviewed with a few families and found one that wanted to hire me and I was interested in. I wrapped things up at home, packed a ton of boxes and shipped them off by UPS, and headed to White Plains, New York. Little did I know what I was getting myself into. I had to end up paying for my flight there and I was really surprised to find that the family wasn't going to pick me up. They had me get on a van that picked numerous people up from the airport. Along the way, they ended up dropping about seven other people off at various places and I was the last one to be dropped off... at a restaurant where I had to call my new nanny family from a pay phone. I had to wait about 20 minutes. Mind you, they didn't have cell phones or electronics then.

After I was picked up, I was taken to the home and it was after 8:00 p.m. They showed me to my room and told me to be up by 6:00

a.m. for my first day. I hadn't met the two children and didn't know where anything was. All I knew was I needed to be up and ready to go, early! That morning when I got up, they were out the door - not showing me anything, but told me they didn't want the TV on, the kids were to play outside, I had to take them to a scheduled group event, come home, play with them, and then make dinner. The youngest took a bottle and they didn't have a microwave; it had to be warmed up. Mmm, what was I to do? I was left with no directions for anything. I called my mom and she helped guide me though a few things.

A few days went by and things were going okay, but not a comfortable feeling whatsoever. It was their daughter's birthday and she was turning three, so I made her a cake. She already was telling me she loved me. So sweet. During all of this newness and trying to learn, they had me start packing up their kitchen because they were going to move. It was SO MUCH thrown at me with no direction. I tried to ask a few questions but seemed to frustrate them. I met a few other nannies and one of them invited me over to meet her family. What a huge difference in the families! I broke down in tears when I told them what was going on. They were shocked that the family I was with didn't spend any time with me or show me around. They knew another family that offered to take me in and be a nanny to their 10-year-old daughter and even pay for me to go to college while I was there. It was an incredible offer. I went back to my original nanny family and decided, I tried this and it wasn't for me.

After a few weeks, I hit my end point, found a one-way ticket home and wrote a check for $630 dollars to just get home. I called UPS, had them come pick up the boxes the next day, and told my nanny family it wasn't working. I couldn't get out of there fast enough. My mom picked me up from the airport at 11:00 pm and I just sobbed. I was glad to be home, but knew I needed to make changes.

I still wonder what would have happened had I gone with the family with the 10-year - old and stayed there for college. It was a decision I had to live with and had to stop playing the "what if" game. I'm glad I had the courage to try something new and experience it. It wasn't what I expected, and it definitely stayed with me. What I can say is, we have nannies ourselves now for our own children and I know how to respect, love and treat them. Just because it wasn't for me didn't mean that I failed at it. I just found out that that job wasn't for me and I was ready to try a different path.

If you're wondering what I did next...I ended up going back to college and auditioned for the auto show where I was hired by Acura. I had no idea again what I was in for, but I had a blast traveling the United States as a narrator and product specialist for a few years. What a great experience! I met a ton of new friends, met some celebrities and traveled to a lot of new states I hadn't been to before.

I left my comfort zone to be a nanny (which didn't work out) but then tried again and found something I loved.

Stand up and face whatever challenge it is. You were born strong and only weakened by your own negative self-talk. Stand up, leave your comfort zone, get the job done and let change be a good thing!

Until then...Don't Coast in Neutral, Positive Shift Ahead

11

Jealousy, How it Affects You and Others

It's amazing how quickly your mood can change, how deep your heart and thoughts can think, and how much one person can affect you.

Jealousy is a human emotion. It is the natural response of a person to something or someone that threatens their social, physical, or emotional holding. Humans have developed the emotion of "jealousy" since primitive times, and it has been like cancer to the society ever since.

Types of jealous people

Though some take jealousy as a positive emotion to build themselves, most of the time it works to bring others down. In either case, it only aids the rat race and does not help the person. If you are not jealous and instead have a set of goals for yourself, you will do a lot better than trying to catch up with someone. We have all been running a race; the race of climbing the ladder first. Being jealous of all the people above us, we forget to look down at all the people we are above. We don't think that they might just be as jealous of us as we are of the people one step above us. Think of all the people who haven't even started climbing the ladder.

Define your success, don't copy others

In the middle of all the mess, we usually forget to look at where we started from, as opposed to where we are today. Think about how many ladders we have climbed. Everyone has their own definition of success, but it changes when we reach it. Even though a $10/hour job might mean success for someone, a million-dollar mansion might be success for someone else, or for the same person after a few decades. The most beloved definition of success to me is the one said by an author,

"If you are doing what you love to do and could still manage to pay the bills, then from my perspective, you are successful."

For some, success could be being with the people you love, in a small cottage, having two meals a day, and spending time with them. So, it is on you—whether you call yourself successful or not; it's you who decides and not the people around you.

Learn to love

When the people around you share their experiences, instead of developing a feeling of jealousy, take pride that they found you to be someone worthy of sharing their experience. If people did not feel jealous of the people around them, the world would be a better place.

Conclusion

In the present society, we all want more and life in general is more competitive. When someone shares their excitement, don't feel as if they are bragging. Be excited with them! Understand that being jealous only pulls you down, threatens your calm state of mind, and reduces your productivity. If being jealous actually pulled you up somewhere, we would have outrun ourselves long ago. Believe in yourself. Trust yourself. Let yourself shine with confidence!

There have been many times when I wished I had what others had, wanted to go to all the cool places that someone else had been. But when I stepped back, I realized that I have so much and have had experiences many others would have liked to have had. All good things will come when it is time, and sometimes it's worth that wait.

We all have and will continuously experience bits of jealousy. Even today at times, I wonder why I wasn't invited to an event or asked to go on a vacation with my friends. When I see friends posting events on social media that I would have loved to have attended, it can immediately put that jealous factor into my head. When that occurs, I look at all the fantastic things I have been doing, the places I just visited, and all my future plans. I don't let it play with my emotions, thoughts or head. I am not going to be jealous, but instead be happy that they get to experience things and I am happy for them. It makes me feel better and doesn't play with my emotions either; leaving me in control of myself. I love me, I love my life and I respect myself.

Until then...Don't Coast in Neutral, Positive Shift Ahead!

12

When Life Gets Tough CTRL+ALT+DEL

It may be a test to see how badly we want something, how hard we will work to get it, and how much stronger we are at the end of it.

What a great concept to think about! Let's face it, life give us challenges, tough times and rough situations. When these times arrive, you must face it. The outcome is all in how you handle it. It's time to reboot and Ctrl + Alt + Del. Here is your Positive Shift Tool Kit.

CONTROL your thoughts

You can have an internal battle with your thoughts. Since we tend to lean towards the negative in tough situations, our thoughts start to play mind games with us and the

71

"what-if" analysis begins. Be in control, and get in the habit of stopping the negative thoughts before they consume your every thought. Try saying: Control, Alt, Delete three times in a row. It will help you from going down that path and having even more negative thoughts. When you say the C+A+D three times, it gives your mind a break and clears your thoughts. Even if you have to say it over and over 100 times, that's okay. Then think of something that makes you happy. It also helps you from saying something you might regret.

ALTER your emotions

You yourself can make your heartrate increase, just with emotions and how you feel. Heartrates drop when emotions are calm and relaxed. They can skyrocket when we let our emotions get to us and make us feel mad, scared or uber-angry. Other people can trigger your emotions, but you don't have to react to them. When you add the thoughts with emotions, it affects us even faster and often leads to a negative outcome which could have been controlled, especially when your initial reaction leads to a sudden impulse. You may not be able to control the situation given, but you can control your emotional outcome.

DELETE your negativity

Even after you say the C+A+D several times, you might battle the urge to go back to the negative thoughts and emotions. STOP IT! It will make you preoccupied with self-doubt. That can't ever result in a WIN-WIN situation. Take action and visualize yourself using the Ctrl + Alt + Del keys. Restart and reboot your thoughts, emotions, and negative impulses. Stop investing in negative thoughts and emotions; instead, invest in altering these thoughts and emotions by practicing positive alternative steps.

Experiencing the negative thoughts, I was challenged and would let them take control of me. I let things get in my head and literally my heartrate would increase, my head would start hurting from stress, and I could feel myself ready to break down in tears. Just by my own internal thoughts! For a period of time, when I would go running by myself, I would start to get the crazy thoughts of something happening to me because of the recent stories I would hear of runners being assaulted, missing or worse. I would run with pepper spray, a knife, and always be aware of my surroundings. I realized I had to redirect what was happening and used the CCD and mantra a bazillion times when running so I could get my miles in. It worked, and I became more relaxed and enjoyed my runs.

I also was challenged with the thoughts of constantly losing my job because of rumors in the company. There were several months during my pharmaceutical years that they were downsizing. I chose to take a different approach and not allow any negative thoughts to take over and drive me insane from an outcome that wasn't in my control. I just kept going strong with my day-to-day work, keeping my mantra close. I had co-workers wonder how and why I wasn't worried. I told them, why worry about something that wasn't in my control? If I sat there and worried for several months and nothing happened, I wasted all those months of feeling that way for nothing and it wasn't worth it. What was going to happen would happen. Only I could control my feelings. Needless to say, I was safe and my job was secure!

Change your outcome. You have nothing to lose and everything to gain by using this Positive Shift Tool Kit!

Until then…Don't Coast in Neutral, Positive Shift Ahead!

13

Imposter Syndrome

You think success is for other people when you work hard and deliver well, but constantly second guessing yourself is exhausting.

Have you recently landed a new job, received a promotion or experienced something else exciting? You feel the rush of excitement for a split second and then...self-doubt when your mind begins its negative self-talk to you. Do you feel like you don't deserve any of it? Well, you are just another person affected by the crippling effects of the imposter syndrome.

Imposter syndrome is a feeling which makes a person feel like a fraud. As if they have tricked someone for their own benefit

77

and gotten success, they shouldn't have in the first place. Most sufferers of the imposter syndrome are sure their achievements and accomplishments are based on pure luck.

Instead of feeling that they were responsible for creating their own success, they feel they have never excelled in anything and do not deserve the rewards that came their way. You, too, may have reached a point in your career where you have felt the tremors of the imposter syndrome.

The bad thing about the imposter syndrome is that you will never be able to fully get rid it, but you can surely reduce the effects of it in your life. There are several types of imposter syndrome, and though each one of them leads to the same results and has more or less the same foundation, the sufferers have a different belief in each of the categories.

To combat the imposter syndrome, the first step is to identify the cause. You need to determine what is crippling your confidence, like running a troubleshooting exercise. Once you have determined the cause, you need to tell it to someone you trust, someone who can get you back on your feet again.

The next step to get over it is to trust the people around you - people who have a hand in bringing you up where you are. Where being a "rugged individualist" helps to boost your confidence, sometimes you just need to accept the fact that people around you have an impact on your success. It prevents the "I got lucky" factor from taking over and also doesn't let your ego run amuck.

I remember feeling this imposter syndrome when I was asked by a chamber to be their keynote speaker for a January kick-off to the year. I was excited and honored that they believed in me enough to not only have me speak, but make it a multi-chamber event and invite other chambers. The event started out being held at their chamber office; however, the response was overwhelming with attendees and they had to move it to a country club. As the number of responses kept coming in, my insecurities rose. We were up to 70 RSVP's now, and I had a severe case of the imposter syndrome... not feeling like I was good enough, smart enough, or could deliver a strong effective message to them. The morning of the event, I saw stars and was light headed. Fear, insecurity and doubt was all over me. I was sweating all over. I begged my sister to come, and she helped me set up. One of my best friends came to support me, as well. She had never heard me speak before. As the event went on and I delivered an impactful presentation, I still felt like I could have done more. My best friend admitted to me after the fact that she was nervous for me and had no idea I could deliver such impactful information. She was beyond impressed. Still, even with the feedback forms giving me rave reviews, I had imposter syndrome.

Overcoming this is not easy and takes a lot of effort. One friend told me to always remember that when I am presenting, I am the expert who knows more about my delivery than the ones listening. What a useful and impactful statement! Since then, my confidence is up and I refuse to allow that imposter syndrome to enter my thoughts.

I also learned that one of the things that helps most in the battle against the imposter syndrome is writing, or rather just fictional writing. There is a truer version of our story and a version we see. Since no one ever saw your story completely, what you saw is the ultimate truth for anyone. So just write it down! Reframe your own story and write each step that brought you here. This will help you recall every achievement you have had over your time; this boosts confidence. You might sometimes overlook tutorials in a video or audio, but what is penned must be true.

The next step is to mind your language. Using phrases like "I think" over "I feel" are going to make you believe you are actually capable of what you have achieved; it wasn't all thrown at you. Though it sounds weird, such passive elements play a vital role. The last step is to mentor someone! Share your knowledge, and eventually you'll learn how much you really know about the subject and all the skills you've been taking for granted.

Until then...Don't Coast in Neutral, Positive Shift Ahead!

14

It's Time to Stop Apologizing

*You don't have to apologize for being you,
love yourself for all that you are.*

Do you find yourself apologizing for
every single thing? This is a sorry habit
indeed! This message is geared to showing
you how awful the 'I'm sorry' habit is. As
humans and especially women, we are guilty
of apologizing for unnecessary things. This is
a terrible habit that can easily be passed on to
impressionable children. Picture apologizing
for the mess in your house to a guest,
apologizing for your child's behavior, for
asking a question, or for being ambushed
while wearing comfy around-the-house
clothes. It really is ridiculous to feel the need
to apologize for things you can't help or

control. This does not, however, mean that apologizing is wrong. You just need to ensure the situation warrants an apology.

Why you should stop this "sorry" habit

Saying "I'm sorry" in situations where it is not warranted sends a message that you are defensive and insecure because you feel bad about yourself for normal things. The word "sorry" should not be used for requesting help, interjecting your opinion or thought into a conversation, or apologizing for everyday situations that are out of your control. The sorry habit - other than making you look defensive and insecure - can also make you lose respect, especially if you are in a position of leadership or attempting to resolve a conflict at home or in the workplace. Saying "sorry" too much makes your apologies meaningless when it really matters.

How the sorry habit affects children

In a nutshell, children mirror our behavior and it is up to us to ensure we are doing it right. The habit of apologizing for everything can be mirrored by children and also sends them a bad message. Over-apologizing is a habit that makes you look weak, guilty, and becomes annoying and irritating. It sets a bad example to children who may take up the habit and also look weak and be plagued by the constant feeling of being in the wrong.

The right way to apologize

In situations where an apology is warranted, apologizing should be done in the right manner. However, if you are unsure as to whether the situation warrants an apology, or if you catch yourself starting to spew out an unwarranted apology, then a good way to combat or circumvent this is to replace the "sorry" with another phrase such as "thanks." That way, rather than saying "I'm sorry that took so long," you say 'thank you for your patience.' Another way to break the sorry habit is by observing silence. This is especially effective in cases where you find yourself saying sorry for when you are confused about the right thing to say. Silence is effective, because it gives you the chance to think of another phrase or figure out the right way to express yourself without apologizing.

I remember first hearing "I'm sorry" a lot when I was in middle school. There was a girl named Ashely who would literally say "I'm sorry" for everything. Somewhere along the line, I picked it up and started saying it for everything - and I mean I said it all the time! It became a bad habit and so hard to control. It took a very long time to stop saying it, and even as an adult would catch myself saying it unnecessarily. As a parent, I hear my daughter saying "I'm sorry" for no real reason and I quickly correct it. She is picking up on when to say it and when not to - to use it when it is truly necessary and needed. I also make comments to people when they say "I'm sorry" when they don't need to – and they appreciate it. Apologizing means more when it is at the right time and is truly meant. Remember that the next time you are apologizing.

Until then…Don't Coast in Neutral, Positive Shift Ahead!

15

Changing Your Mindset: Using "I AM" Positively

I AM ~ two of the most powerful words for what you put after them shapes your reality.

I wish, I want, I need...we all have said this several times and maybe even multiple times a day. After we say or think this, our minds start to drift off to the negative because those wishes, wants and needs aren't being met or they aren't happening fast enough. Ever wonder why that is? Of course, it's you!

You are the creator of making those things happen or not making them come to you. I'm going to put this in the simplest terms for you and want you to think about this the next time you say those things. I'll also tell you how to redirect what you're saying in the correct way.

Here goes…if you find a lamp, rub it, a genie comes out and asks what your three wishes are, you expect it to happen because you asked for it. I mean seeing the genie come out of the bottle is proof that it is magical; therefore, it must be true. As the saying goes, you don't get wet from saying the word "water." You have to drink the water or feel the water to know it's real. You breathe air even though you don't "see" the air. Hopefully, you're getting the idea.

I know this from experience and have seen the forthcoming of being "lucky" just by my words, by feeling it and believing it. I went on a golf outing as part of a foursome. One golfer I knew and the other two I didn't. I wrenched my back that morning but still went golfing. I said, "I am" going to have the best golf game ever. That I did! I even had them video me, because I knew no one would believe I could hit the ball as far and as straight as I did. During the golf game, they had a putt-putt challenge you could partake in for $20. The three other golfers offered to pay for it if I did. I said, "Thanks for offering, but I'm good." They really wanted to do something for me for bringing them golfing. I told them that if they insisted, I would be grateful if they were to purchase some raffle tickets for me during the dinner portion of the event. Nine tickets were waiting for me. When we walked up to a random table to sit down, I blurted out, "Well, here is the winning table! Right here! "I am" a winner!"

I was so excited and felt it, believed it and knew I would win. Long story short, four of us won twice and everyone else at the table of 10 won at least once! (Except for the one golfer who didn't buy tickets). Since then, in less than one month, I have proclaimed "I am" lucky and have won a free nights' stay at a hotel, a raffle basket at an event, purchased two scratch off tickets and won on both of those, and finally, found out that I won the Governor's Service Award for Mentor of the Year!

"I Am" is your own personal genie! You rub your own words and thoughts to make things come to you. Negativity will cancel out your positive streak, so don't let it get in the way of your "I Am." It breaks down to this...When you are saying "I am," you are declaring it to be a fact. If you say, "I am overweight" or "I am sick" or "I am tired" or "I am depressed" or "I am stupid" or "I am poor," you get the point, then the "Genie, aka your own wishes," is giving you what you want more of - your "I am."

Change your Mindset! You have nothing to lose and everything to gain by using this Positive Shift Tool Kit!

Until then...Don't Coast in Neutral, Positive Shift Ahead!

16

Don't be Afraid of Change and Challenge Yourself

Authenticity: Knowing who you are and being brave enough to live it.

I worked my way through many unknown territories and did what most couldn't or wouldn't by challenging my career choices and not following the continued flow of a certain area of expertise. I like random information and was trying to find my happiness in what I was supposed to be doing. This led me down an unusual career path.

Many tears were shed through this process, but there were also many incredible adventures and experiences. More happy and fun times than the tears, being on my hands and knees not knowing what I was doing, where I was going and how I was going to get out of my dark hole. Lots of ups and downs. I learned I may not be in control of a situation that presents itself, but I was and always will be in control of how I handle my outcome.

While finishing high school, I did a co-op job at the hospital being a "transportation runner" of patients, meds and various items for about four years. Worked at the mall as a sales person, department manager in a large department store, a manager at a sunglass place. Was a hostess with the mostest at a restaurant where the manager crossed the line and I left, calling an hour later to let them know I would not be returning. Next thing you know, I became a nanny and left for New York. Came home and decided it was time for college. I worked full-time while getting my degree. At some point landed a job doing the auto shows as a narrator and product specialist, continuing to get my college degree.

After a few years of the auto shows, I landed a job as a front desk person and worked hard to move up in the company. Four years later 911 happened and my position was eliminated. Took the opportunity and finished up my one remaining semester of college and received my BA in Communications from Oakland University. Now what! Next thing I know, I was a fourth-grade teacher at a charter school for two years. Received a call from a pharmaceutical company, interviewed and landed that job. For the next four years, I was ranking number 1 in sales and doing well as a pharmaceutical and vaccine representative and loving life.

I was making great money as a pharma rep and wasn't looking, yet I had just had my daughter and was feeling like a change. Lo and behold, six months after my daughter was born, I was recruited by a hospital only three miles from my home. This hospital job was wonderful and I woke up loving work every day. I had the most amazing boss to work with and worked with physicians for years. This is where I started to realize what I could accomplish with the help of an amazing boss, mentor and President of the hospital, Lynn. She saw my potential and after two years of working there, nominated me to attend the hospital's Leadership Academy, which I did and completed! Continuing to grow as the Director of Physician Relations and Recruitment in the company I loved, I was feeling great about my success.

Years later, Lynn left and a new president was in place. Karen was the former COO of the hospital, and she knew what I could do and more. I continued working hard and accepting new challenges. Karen gave me a chance to grow once more with heavier duties as the Director of Business Development and Community Relations. I grew more and became a member of the Administration and C-suite team. I was on top of the world and doing incredible things. Then, our hospital was bought out and a new team was being brought in. Meaning, the A-Team and C-Suite team were being eliminated. One-month shy of my 10-year anniversary, my position was eliminated. I knew it was coming and was one step ahead. While removing all of my personal belongings from my office, I ran into the HR Director who wanted to meet with me to let me know. She was surprised and a bit shaky when she saw me with my box, walking to my car I already had parked at the front entrance. With respect, they didn't escort me out, just had me sign papers in my office and off I went. Holding my head high, I made calls and celebrated with champagne and some great friends knowing there was something more for me to learn.

I kept it positive and once again, was recruited by a home health and hospice company. That was short-lived, only putting a year and half in before I received a call from a recruiter. Are you ready for this, a "funeral business." It took me from September to December to make the decision. I became their

Director of Business Development at one of
their locations. Over the next month, I learned
things I never knew existed. It blew my mind
and gave me a whole appreciation for life,
what you choose to do with it and how short
life truly is. Make note of that statement!
Since then, I've come in contact with
numerous community members, friends, and
families who are open to listen and hear they
have a choice to have the last word and
choose their own legacy. Let's not be afraid to
talk about this. I even had one person say,
"well, if I have to funeral plan or think about
this type of thing, then I wouldn't want to
plan with anyone else as you have taken a
positive twist and it makes me feel much more
comfortable."

I share this with you because if you are
shy, fearful and just plain don't like change,
ask yourself why and what are you afraid of?
I'm not a fan of change either because it is
hard, scary, challenging, and so much more.
What I can share is, I have life experiences

which have made me who I am today. I
found my passion that was always there but
needed the experience to understand life
better. These job and career choices allow me
to connect and understand my coaching
clients. Those choices allow me to value and
understand businesses, communities and all
the amazing jobs out there that no one knows
about. They also have taught me to be
adaptable and to believe in myself. Believe I
can and will do anything I want to.

I will share my personal mantra my dad
and I created. Not only do I say it multiple
times a day, but my amazing children
Samantha and Zachary have learned it and
say it when they are having a rough day, a
scary nightmare or when they are feeling
negative. They turn their negative feelings
into positive ones and usually laugh because
they end it with...I BELIEVE, I RECEIVE!

My personal mantra: I am a very powerful
magnet. I ask and command that all good
things the universe has to offer, that are for

my best good, come to me now. So be it, it is done now, in divine order. Amen and thank you! (I BELIEVE, I RECEIVE!)

I leave you with this. If you try a new path and you're struggling, that is okay. It does not mean you failed or did not try hard enough; it just means it is not the right path for you. At least you took that leap of faith and tried something! You gained some knowledge from it and are ready to try something new until you find the right fit. Jump around and find you and find your passion!

What are you going to challenge yourself with now? I'd love to hear!

Until then...Don't Coast in Neutral, Positive Shift Ahead!

Conclusion

If you see the commonality in these chapters, it's all about what we have created in our own minds and fears of the unknown. Most of these negativities are based on fear. Your own internal fear. **F.E.A.R.** **F**alse **E**vidence **A**ppearing **R**eal (how my dad tells it to me).

Remember, you have to go through the tough and difficult struggles to understand and grow. Work on you. Never become complacent; life is work, and you should never stop challenging yourself.

You also have to take care of your health. You are no hero by going to work sick, brushing aside your ailments as if they're nothing. No one gets a prize or award for having a disease and avoiding it. Thing about that word, disease…Dis Ease. It's not fair to your family, children, spouse if you don't take care of yourself. You're disrespecting yourself and them by not getting something checked out. You were given feelings of "discomfort" for a reason, so be alert to what your body is trying to tell you. You can't perform well at work or home if you don't.

Something else to keep in mind about your job or career. If you're doing something for eight hours a day that you can't stand doing, you're getting ill, having headaches, it is time for a change. Again, don't be complacent. There is something more out there for you. Your life is too short to be miserable and not get what you want. Just know…whatever it takes to get you where you want to be, do what you love and be happy, is all inside of you. You and you alone can make that happen if you're willing to invest in yourself, believe in yourself, and love yourself.

Goal Setting Time

Take action NOW! Today, as you finish reading this. Go get a piece of paper and fold it in half. This paper is for you and you alone. Not to be shared with anyone but your own eyes. Write down three goals. Not dreams, but three goals that are in arm's length, - things you have been wanting but never took action on. Write down those three goals now.

Why

Write down a "why" for your goals. One why for each of your three goals.

How

Write down "how" for your goals. How are going to achieve those goals? Again, one how for each of your three goals.

Turn your paper over.

Cancel Clear Delete (CCD)

Write cancel, clear, delete on the left side of your paper. Now put 3x's. You will say the CCD. three times when you get a negative thought in your head that is getting in the way of your goals.

Mantra

In the middle of the page, write a mantra. Most of us don't have one, so I'm offering you two simple ones that will work until you come up with one that fits your personality.

Mantra: Every day in every way, "I AM" better, Better, BETTER!

Mantra: "I AM" awesome, successful and smart. I succeed at what I put my mind to!

Happy Place

Next step, on the right side of your paper, put down a happy place that is meaningful to you. One that you can get emotional about. Feel the sun on your face, smell the fresh cut grass, hear the ocean waves. Whatever it is, put it down so you can go there when you need to stop the negative thoughts.

CCD, Mantra, Happy Place all Put Together

Saying, thinking and feeling those three steps stops your mind, thoughts and emotions from continuing to take you down the negative path. It makes you think about something other than the negative and refocuses your thoughts so you can continue moving forward with your goals and your everyday life.

You are in control and have the steps to shift into gear and go for what you desire. You and you alone.

Until then...Don't Coast in Neutral, Positive Shift Ahead!

3 Goals Example

How to Fill Out your 3 Goals Worksheet

My personal example below on my 3 (arm's length) goals.

3 **Goals**

1) Be better organized and more focused.
2) Block time for family, children and friends.
3) Complete Book: Positive Shift Ahead!

3 **Why** You Want	3 **Steps How** to Get There
1) So I can be less stressed & not so lost in my daily commitments.	1) Write daily TO DO list. Set alarms on my phone. Prioritize tasks. Say NO without an explanation.
2) Sometimes I feel disconnected from the most important people in my life.	2) Schedule family nights, dates & be spontaneous with my family.
3) Passion for motivating & educating others.	3) Block one hour a day in the evenings to write.

Fill in your own 3 Goals

3 Goals Blank Grid

Make a copy of this grid below or take a half sheet of paper and make your own.

3 **Goals**

1)
2)
3)

3 **Why** You Want	3 **Steps How** to Get There
1)	1)
2)	2)
3)	3)

CCD, Mantra and Your Happy Place Put All Together

Back of Goal Sheet

This is what the back of your 3 Goals would look like.

CCD, Mantra & Happy Place

CCD	Mantras	Happy Place
CANCEL	I AM AWESOME,	I go to this "Happy Place"
CLEAR	SUCCESSFUL AND SMART!	and visualize this:
DELETE	I SUCCEED AT WHAT	
CANCEL	I PUT MY MIND TO!	
CLEAR		
DELETE	~	
	EVERYDAY IN EVERY WAY	
CANCEL	I AM	
CLEAR	Better, Better, BETTER!	
DELETE		
	~	
Say 3x's	I BELIEVE! I RECEIVE!	

A Lasting Thought

I'm leaving you with one more Positive Shift Ahead tool. It's the "I Have a Choice" poem. I wrote it when I was a teacher. The kids read it every day, and they ended up memorizing it and loving it. It was helpful to each student and continues to be helpful to others. This poem is used in my motivational and strategy speeches as well as my personal coaching.

Life is about choices and what we do with those choices. How you wake up, the choices you make, getting caught on something, making things right, thinking about your day and making goals for tomorrow.

YOU ARE AMAZING!

I HAVE A CHOICE!

When I wake up in the morning,
"I" have a choice of having a good or bad attitude.

When I make a mistake,
"I" have a choice of blowing it off or learning from it.

When I get in trouble for doing wrong,
"I" have a choice of getting upset because I got caught,
or listening and learning how to make it right.

When I hurt or make fun of someone,
"I" have a choice to feel the guilt or admit I was wrong
and apologize.

When I go to bed at night,
"I" have a choice to fall asleep quickly or
think about my day and make goals for myself,
to make for a better tomorrow.

I have a Choice!!

By: Stacie René

Stacie René

Thank you for Reading Positive Shift Ahead!

I appreciate that you chose this book to learn some simple but effective shifting tools.

If you want to learn more, or to connect with me, please visit my company's website here: https://www.positiveshiftahead.com/ or connect with me on my personal site here: https://www.stacierene.com/.

Thank you again for reading this book and please remember it is always an arm's length away to pick it back up for some quick reminder tips.

I can't wait to hear from you!

Stacie René

Author's Request

Your Amazon Review

Reviews are very important for authors. Not only do they provide great feedback, but they help us write more books. They also give potential readers insights into how the book will help them. Would you be so kind as to leave this book, Positive Shift Ahead, a review on Amazon?

It doesn't take very long and only a few sentences are needed and very much appreciated!

I look forward to hearing how this book may have helped you personally or professionally. Thank you for your extra time in providing a review. I know time is of value.

Thank you again for reading this book, writing an Amazon review, and giving so much of your valuable time!

Stacie René

About the Author

Stacie René

Stacie René Zotkovich, a Michigan native, has been impacting the lives of individuals for decades with her strategic leadership and life coaching programs. Her approach, rooted in energizing individuals to rediscover their passion, assists them in fine-tuning their behaviors to promote a sense of purpose and excellence in their day-to-day lives, ultimately empowering them to find the path to reach their goals.

The one-of-a-kind tactics Stacie uses unlock each individual's unlimited potential and allow them to confidently pursue their personal goals. In her sessions, made up of individual and small groups, she uses basic exercises to help attendees understand where they have opportunities for growth or improvement, develop social and mental skills, and initiate positive behaviors that will allow them set realistic goals. Together, they explore thoughts of the empowered mindsets, behaviors and perspectives that drive performance forward, and learn to acknowledge and celebrate their accomplishments along the way. Stacie also provides all clients with a specialized assessment that allows them to better understand themselves and provides guidance on developing strategies for long-term success.

Stacie served as President of the West Bloomfield Chamber of Commerce and maintains involvement with over 100 charitable organizations, creating many of the supporting events that benefit citizens, organizations and groups throughout Michigan. She continues with her passion of coaching, educating, empowering, and creating a positive emotional balance for individuals. She is a former Mrs. Michigan United States in 2014 and former Mrs. Michigan USA Universal 2016. Stacie is a frequent motivational, strategy and keynote speaker, sharing her personal experiences with a goal to reveal that we are all alike and united by similar struggles and circumstances and that success is within your grasp.

Stacie also holds the following accolades:

- Governors Service Award for Mentor of the Year
- Greater West Bloomfield Leadership Award

- Person of the Week, Inspiring & Providing to others in the Community, Award from GWB Civic Center TV
- Best of Michigan Businesses Transformative Leader Award
- Esteemed Women of Michigan Award
- Community Excellence Award for Spirit of the Community
- Honored by the State of Michigan for her leadership and community involvement and was presented with a United States and Michigan flag that was flown over the state capital in Lansing in her honor
- Outstanding Citizen Award

She admits her accolades wouldn't be possible without the support of her husband Craig, her two children, Samantha and Zachary, and her close and supportive friends.

Impacting Others

Testimonies

Stacie's proof of positive impact is what makes her efforts unique - how she helps so many organizations. By using her own stories, successes, and hardships, Stacie continuously inspires and motivates her audiences and program participants.

However, it is often better to view an individual through the eyes of others, so here are a few comments from the community:

"Stacie has helped me to stay positive even when I was at my worst. Her positive words, and motivation really helped me to strengthen myself when I thought I couldn't."

Audrey Ray
Country Music Singer / Songwriter

Stacie René

"Stacie didn't have to take me under her wing nor care, but she did and for that I'm grateful. I could have sent this privately, but I really wanted people to know whom she was and is when no one is looking and she had nothing to gain. That's character and a servant's heart. That's her and that is good."

Shaylett Stuckey - Mrs. Michigan America 2015 Entrepreneur & Small Business Advocate

"It's amazing how much I have been able to accomplish with my business since I started working with Stacie. I have more confidence at networking events. I have a much more positive outlook on the success of my business. I'm reaching for higher goals and doing things that I never dreamed I was capable of doing! Stacie, Thank you so much for your support and expertise!"

Anita Rogan Jennings
Business Owner and Entrepreneur

126

"Stacie knows how to engage an audience. She spends just the right amount of time, briefly touching on the experiences and struggles that helped shape her mindset, which makes her relatable. Her powerful and thought-provoking presentations not only gets people thinking, it gets them DOING! Stacie provides a realistic and gradual approach to The Positive Shift," by breaking things down into bite-size steps that are attainable."

Emily Taucher
Marketing & Sponsorship Director
Twelve Oaks Mall

"Stacie is one of the first people I think of when I need a push outside of my comfort zone. She has a contagious confidence that helps to put me at ease in decision-making and follow though boldly. I trust her opinion and thoughtfulness completely."

Trinity Pearson
Mrs. Tennessee America 2018

127

"I have to thank Stacie for sharing some terrific counsel, encouragement and specific action items to those in attendance at the event. It was a delightful gathering and I have begun working on one of my NEW goals for this year already thanks to her challenge! Appreciate her transparency, wisdom and professionalism."

Diane Logan

"For many years, I always scoffed at motivational speakers. There was never enough time in the day, let alone enough time for me or to process things that were stressful or seemingly impossible. I didn't want to hear the "sunshine and rainbows" speech as I had heard a thousand times before. Truth be told, I was a skeptic until I met Stacie. Her passion shines through very brightly almost instantaneously. What I appreciated most about Stacie is that she is honest. A realist. Stacie conveyed to us that the world won't always be "sunshine and rainbows," and some days it rains hard. But that's okay. She has a way of passing her determination to not give up and her strong-willed way of thinking through to her speakers. I watched the audience's gears turning as she constantly provoked the thought of "What can I do better?" and then most importantly "How do I get there?" In less than an hour, I watched her teach others to slow down, breathe, and figure out what was most important for them and how they can accomplish those ideas. She taught us all that the impossible really is possible."

Stevie Yeager

"Stacie offered support and guidance at a time I needed it most, when you could have easily used the situation for personal gain. It takes a special kind of woman to put the needs of others first, offer genuine insight and hand to hold. I admired you before, but now I truly look up to you. I am so grateful for you!"

Jessica Brown

"Stacie, I need to let you know how much I enjoyed the presentation you did. To be honest, I wasn't all that excited about getting up so early to trek out to an early morning workshop in the middle of such a cold snowy week. However, I am so glad I did!

You have so much to share. It is obvious you love of what you do and your enthusiasm is contagious. Your presentation was motivating, engaging, educational and insightful. Daily, I pause and think about some of the tidbits you shared that help me to stay focused.

One last thing please, please add me to your mailing list so I can be sure to take advantage of future opportunities."

Lynn Lipman
Monat Global Market Partner
Hempworx Affiliate

Positive Shift Ahead!

Until then…
Don't Coast in Neutral,
Positive Shift Ahead!

Stacie René

Positive Shift Ahead!

Positive Shift Ahead!

Positive Shift Ahead!

Made in the
USA
Middletown, DE